# DYING YOU DESTROYED OUR DEATH

# DYING YOU DESTROYED OUR DEATH

## Prayers and Reflections to Comfort those who Mourn

Edited by
Andrew G. McGrady

VERITAS

First published 1992 by
Veritas Publications
7-8 Lower Abbey Street
Dublin 1

5 4 3 2 1

ISBN 1 85390 255 0

*Nihil obstat*
Patrick Jones
Censor Deputatis

British Library Cataloguing
in Publication Data.
A catalogue record for
this book is available
from the British Library.

Cover design by Joe Gervin
Printed in the Republic of Ireland
by Criterion Press Ltd, Dublin

## ACKNOWLEDGMENTS

The advice and encouragement in the preparation of this booklet provided by the Very Rev. Mgr Sean Swayne PP, Rev. John Terry CC, Rev. Brian Magee CM and Rev. Donal Neary SJ, is gratefully acknowledged.

Andrew G. McGrady

# CONTENTS

## PART TWO: PRAYERS FOR THOSE WHO MOURN

# HOW TO USE THIS BOOK

When a loved one dies we receive many letters from friends offering us their support in our pain and sorrow. This booklet is like such a letter. It comes from people who know from their own experience the anguish that follows the death of a spouse, a parent, a child, a brother or sister, a relative or other close friend. It is offered to you in a spirit of solidarity during your time of mourning.

To mourn the loss of a loved one is natural. It is a sign of the love we shared with the one who has died. It is natural to feel pain, hurt, numbness and even anger. Death forces us to ask the hardest questions concerning this life and the next, and it is a time when it is hardest to find answers which make sense. Yet Jesus taught that those who mourn are blessed because they are close to the kingdom of God. The time following the death of a loved one is therefore a time when we may wish to turn to God in prayer. Sometimes, however, we find it hard to find the words, or to remember prayers which we thought we knew. This booklet is a resource to help you, and your family, to pray during your time of mourning.

The booklet is in two parts. The first part provides a set of daily prayers and reflections for you to use during the month following the funeral of your loved one. Each week of the month has a slightly different focus to reflect the differing moods of our journey through grief. Each daily reflection will allow you to put words on your experience of grief and pain, and offers you the consolation and hope of the gospel of Christ Jesus. Each session begins with a short opening prayer, which is the same for each day of the week. A short biblical text, and a reflection upon it, follow. Finally there is a short concluding prayer, often taken from the

*Order of Christian Funerals* approved for use in Ireland (OCFI). The reading and reflection provided for Day 31 is intended to be used for the day on which the Month's Mind Mass is celebrated. It is of course possible to use the reflections at any time, or over a much longer period than a month. Mourning is not limited to a given period of time, and the journey in grief is different for each one of us; indeed, in a real sense we will grieve for the rest of our lives. But the onset of grieving is a time when we need particular support.

The second part of the book contains a wide selection of individual prayers which can be used at any time. Many popular prayers, as well as some psalms and devotions, including the Rosary, are provided. Prayers for family members who have died, prayers for various moments during the funeral, and prayers to cover the many circumstances surrounding the death of our loved ones, are also included.

You can use this book by yourself or as a means of helping others close to you to pray. The daily prayers and reflections last about ten minutes and can be used for morning or evening prayer, or during a visit to a church. They can of course be used in any quiet place, be it a mount- ain walk, a city park, a kitchen while a meal is cooking, or an empty office. Other prayers are for use when visiting the grave in which the remains of your loved one have been placed, or on an anniversary of your loved one's death.

At this time of sorrow open your heart to the Lord. He shares your grief and longs to walk with you along the way. Only in God can your troubled soul find rest, from him comes our salvation.

Andrew G. McGrady

## Part One

# DAILY PRAYERS
# AND REFLECTIONS

# WEEK 1

# MY GOD, MY GOD,
# WHY HAVE YOU FORSAKEN ME?

## INTRODUCTION TO THE WEEK

> Out of the depths I cry to you, O Lord,
> Lord, hear my voice!
> O let your ears be attentive
> to the voice of my pleading.

*Psalm 130*

The death of our loved one is a painful experience. Death always comes as a shock, be it due to natural causes or tragic circumstances, and is accompanied by a sense of numbness. Our feelings are confused – a sense of loss and sadness, and feelings of loneliness and isolation, may be intermingled with feelings of anger and denial and with depression and physical tiredness. We may try to avoid these emotions, or to deny that they exist. We may hide the tears of anguish welling up within us. If we are to cope with such grief we must first acknowledge that it exists. There is no detour around the hill of Calvary; the cross must be carried, but, once carried, it eventually leads to the resurrection.

Take courage. Be our faith weak or strong, wavering or steady, now is the time to turn to Christ, our Lord and our Saviour. Because Jesus 'loved much' he grieved and wept openly for his loved one, Lazarus. Jesus understands our grief for our loved one because he shares that grief. He hears our anguished prayer, he eases the hurt of our hearts, and offers to share the load of our loss.

It can be hard to pray at this time; it may be difficult to find the words. God may seem absent. 'Surely,' we ask ourselves, 'if he had been nearby our loved one would not have died.' But God is with us, he is listening, though in our sorrow we may find it hard to hear him.

May these daily reflections help you to put words on your anguish, to share your sorrow with the Lord, and to experience the peace that only God can give. May the God of all consolation open your heart to his Word. May you find light in a time of darkness and faith in a time of doubt. Know that the Lord Jesus walks with you along the way, if only you can recognise him. He will comfort you with his promise:

> Blessed are those who mourn,
> for they shall be comforted.

*(Matthew 5:4)*

### Opening Prayer

In the name of the Father and of the Son,
and of the Holy Spirit.
Amen.

Lord Jesus, you console those who are in distress; draw near to us and dry our tears.
Lord have mercy.

*(OCFI 222 adapted)*

Lord Jesus, gentle Shepherd who brings rest to our souls, give peace to N. for ever:
Christ have mercy.

*(OCFI 95)*

Lord Jesus, many other friends and members of our families have gone before us and await your kingdom. Grant them an everlasting home.
Lord have mercy.

(OCFI 177 adapted)

**Reading and Reflection**
*(see separate days)*

**Concluding Prayer**

We pray as Jesus taught us:

Our Father...

Merciful Lord,
you know the anguish of our sorrow,
and the pain of our loss.
Hear our prayers as we cry out to you in our need,
and strengthen our hope in your lasting goodness.

(OCFI 225 adapted)

Into your hands, O Lord,
we humbly entrust  N.
In this life you embraced him/her with your tender love:
deliver him/her now from every evil
and bid him/her enter eternal rest.
May the love of God and the peace of the Lord Jesus Christ,
bless and console us
and gently wipe every tear from our eyes:
in the name of the Father, and of the Son,
and of the Holy Spirit.

Amen.

(OCFI 59B)

# DAY 1

## Scripture Reading

My God, my God, why have you forsaken me?
O my God, I call by day and you give no reply;
I call by night and I find no peace.

*(Psalm 22:1a, 2; Mark 15:34)*

## Reflection

How alone and numb I feel. It seems an eternity since I was
peaceful and contented, yet it is only a short while. These
last few pain-filled days and restless nights are so blurred. I
am drained of all energy, tired and sore, a veil of hurt and
loss lies between me and my friends. As I start each day I
expect to find my dear one there; I expect us to still be
together. But the reality is painfully different, and I seem to
have to remind myself that death has shattered our lives.
Will we ever be able talk together again, or to share a laugh,
or to hold each other in our gaze again?

So many people, relations and friends, neighbours and
unexpected callers, have come to support me, yet even in
the midst of company I feel alone and the heartache
remains. Father, how true your Son's words from the cross
are, I feel forsaken and restless. You helped Jesus in his time
of anguish, you can help me too. Soften this aching pain of
loss; let me trust in you and know your caring presence in
the endless days ahead.

## DAY 2

### Scripture Reading

Jesus said:

"Come to me, all you who labour and are overburdened, and I will give you rest. Shoulder my yoke and learn from me, for I am gentle and humble in heart, and you will find rest for your souls. Yes, my yoke is easy and my burden light."

*(Matthew 11:28-30)*

### Reflection

Another day has passed, seconds dripping through the endless hour-glass of sorrow. Tomorrow has become today. Fleeting memories of the good times we shared together disturb my waking and sleeping hours. I feel helplessly and hopelessly alone. I thought the dawn would never come, but when it came it shone only on a yawning absence. I am weary of this restless grief that denies me comfort and rest.

Lord Jesus, your warm inviting words of comfort seem so far-fetched. This burden of sorrowing, this time of brokenness, leaves me numb inside, wanting to deny reality. You knew the pain of grieving when Joseph died; you saw the sorrow in your mother's face. Because you knew, you could open your heart in compassion to the widow of Naim when she lost her only son after losing her husband. I feel so overburdened, Lord, give me rest. Embrace me in your arms and grant me peace.

## Day 3

### Scripture Reading

Near the cross of Jesus stood his mother and his mother's sister, Mary the wife of Clopas, and Mary of Magdala. Seeing his mother and the disciple whom he loved standing near her, Jesus said to his mother, "Woman, this is your son". Then to the disciple he said, "This is your mother". And from that hour the disciple made a place for her in his home.

*(John 19: 25-27)*

### Reflection

When Jesus died on Calvary his mother, Mary, and the beloved John, were close by. Other true friends were there with them in their moments of grief, reaching out to support them. Throughout his life Jesus had brought solace and consolation to many who suffered. As his living gave way to his dying he still enabled those who were grieving to reach out and support each other. Through such support they would eventually experience peace.

Lord, my loss has made me withdraw into myself, burying my sorrow deep within. At first I thought no one could help, yet there have been moments when the care and mere presence of others has eased my ache. Through such others your healing love has been brought to me. But I must be aware that these friends, who show me such love and care, are grieving also. Give me the strength to be there for them too, just as you asked Mary and John to be there for each other.

# DAY 4

## Scripture Reading

On arriving, Jesus found that Lazarus had been in the tomb for four days already. Bethany is only about two miles from Jerusalem, and many Jews had come to Martha and Mary to sympathise with them over their brother. When Martha heard that Jesus had come she went to meet him. Mary remained sitting in the house. Martha said to Jesus, "If you had been here, my brother would not have died."

*(John 11:17-21)*

## Reflection

The Bethany family of Martha and Mary were comforted by many friends and neighbours. Their words show that they were upset, even angry, with the Lord; disappointed that the one who restored to life both the widow of Naim's son, and the twelve-year-old daughter of Jairus, had not been there for Lazarus.

Lord, did you feel guilt that you were not there when Lazarus died? Death may make us blame ourselves for many things. Such anger and guilt can destroy us.

Lord, you listened to the pain of Martha and Mary. Listen to me as I share my innermost thoughts and feelings. Help me to trust in your presence and experience your peace in this time of anguish.

# DAY 5

## Scripture Reading

This is the false argument the godless use,
"We came into being by chance
and afterwards shall be as though we had never been.
In time, our name will be forgotten,
nobody will remember what we have done."

*(Wisdom 2:2-4)*

We want you to be quite certain about those who have fallen asleep, to make sure that you do not grieve about them, as others do who have no hope.

*(1 Thessalonians 4:13-14)*

## Reflection

If life was just due to chance, and if death was really the end, how utterly hopeless life would be. What a precious gift is faith. While death envelops us in sadness, we still have the firm conviction that our loved ones, though departed, live on with God who is infinite in love and mercy.

With what faith St Paul describes death, as a falling asleep, as a being at peace after the ups and downs of life. We look forward in hope to sharing eternity with those we love in an unbroken communion of love with the Lord. And while we wait we know that the ties of friendship and affection, which knitted us together on this earth, do not in fact unravel with death.

Lord, replace my despair with hope. Let me always cherish the undying bonds of love between yourself, my loved one and myself. One day may we be united in your peace.

# DAY 6

## Scripture Reading

The Lord consoles his people,
is taking pity on his afflicted ones.
For they were saying
"The Lord has abandoned me,
the Lord has forgotten me."
Can a woman forget her baby at the breast,
feel no pity for the child she has borne?
Even if these were to forget,
I shall not forget you.

*(Isaiah 49:13-15)*

## Reflection

In these troubled days what consoling and hope-filled words Isaiah speaks. God's love is tender and sustaining. Can there be a more true image of total love and trust than that of a new mother with her young baby at her breast?

Lord, I feel forgotten, I fear being abandoned. I need to know that you are there, that you will always be close to me. Touch me again and again with your sustaining and healing presence. Never let me forget that you will never forget my loved one, and that you will never forget me.

# DAY 7

## Scripture Reading

When the Sabbath was over, Mary of Magdala, Mary the mother of James, and Salome, bought spices with which to go and anoint the body of Jesus. And very early in the morning of the first day of the week they went to the tomb when the sun had risen.

*(Mark 16:1-2)*

## Reflection
The cruel death of Jesus on the cross, and the hasty burial of his remains in the tomb, must have left Mary of Magdala and the other women in a wilderness of shock, pain and fear. Yet the dawn of a new day brought new courage, courage to face the lifeless body of their Lord and to anoint it as a loving personal farewell.

Lord, like these women, I, too, have brought the lifeless body of my loved one for burial. I did so in tears, silent or visible. As the days pass I, too, return to the place where my loved one been laid to rest. As I do so, help me to know that life is changed, not ended, and that we do not bury people, only their physical remains. Let me begin to lift my eyes from the grave of my loved one, to look into the rising light of a new dawn, sensing the miracle of the birth in each new day.

# WEEK 2

# IN THE FACE OF DEATH WE PROCLAIM: JESUS IS THE RESURRECTION AND THE LIFE

## INTRODUCTION TO THE WEEK

Jesus chose one of the most poignant of times to make a key statement about himself. At a funeral, when the family were mourning a brother, he said, 'I am the resurrection'. Our belief in the resurrection of Jesus does not allow us to ignore the reality of the grave, or to deny the reality of physical death. Our belief in resurrection is founded in the harsh reality of death and bereavement, but enables us to see deeper into this mystery.

Bereavement is an experience which teaches us about ourselves and about the mystery of human life. We learn about our ways of surviving loneliness and loss, we discover strengths in ourselves that we did not know we had. We know the beauty of the bonds of love, and we know their bitterness. We discover our dependencies on others, and our fragilities and weaknesses in coping with the awful tragedy of death.

For death is ever a tragedy, always leaving heartache in its path. Surrounded as it is with hope and regret, love and grudges, confusion and faith, it can bring out the best in our humanity, or it can leave us confused in grief, without energy, hope or initiative.

It is worth remembering that for the Christian, death is not just a single moment but a process that begins during life. In Baptism we journey through death with Christ and begin to share his risen life as we strive to die to sin and selfishness. The daily struggle to let go of that which is sinful, to surrender the self, to trust the other, is a form of dying to self-centredness that reaches finality at the moment of physical death. After such a life, death itself can be the free and final personal act of self-surrender into the love of God, a yielding up of everything we own and are into the welcoming arms of God. In this sense, death is a homecoming, a return to God who in the first instance loved us into existence and at death receives us back into eternal life.

This week's prayer and reflections are based on Jesus' own journey of death. He faced death longing for the resurrection. We cannot say he knew how it would happen. He faced death without much other consolation than that he would throw himself into the loving arms of his Father. That was enough for him. We hope and pray it will be enough for us. Our dead ones are in the arms of God: may they lead us too into the presence of God. At this most sorrowful of times let us turn to Christ Jesus with confidence and faith in the power of his cross and resurrection (*OCFI 95*).

**Opening prayer**

In the name of the Father and of the Son,
and of the Holy Spirit.
Amen.

Risen Lord, pattern of our life for ever:
  Lord, have mercy.

*(OCFI 95)*

Lord Jesus, bless us who mourn and who are in pain:
  Christ, have mercy.

*(OCFI 95  adapted)*

Lord, in baptism N. was joined to you. Lead him/her now
through the waters of death:
  Lord, have mercy.

*(OCFI 177 adapted)*

**Reading and Reflection**
*(see separate days)*

**Concluding Prayer**

Let us pray as Jesus taught us:

Our Father...

Lord God,
at this time of sorrow
let us find in your Son,
comfort in our sadness,
certainty in our doubt,
and courage to live through each day.

*(OCFI 97B adapted)*

In the waters of baptism
N. died with Christ and rose with him to new life.
May he/she now complete that journey and
share his eternal life.

(*OCFI 188 adapted*)

May the God of all consolation
bring us comfort and peace,
in the name of the Father, and of the Son,
and of the Holy Spirit.
Amen.

(*OCFI 241B*)

## Day 8

### Scripture Reading

The two angels at the empty tomb of Jesus said to
the women
"Why look among the dead for someone who is alive?
He is not here, he has risen."

*(Luke 24: 5-6)*

### Reflection
These are the questions we ask in times of bereavement:
Why was he taken and not another?
Why did she suffer so much?
Why look to heaven when I'm left behind on earth?
Why look to God when he has taken my loved one away?

It is good to be as honest with your questions as was the
angel! Let your heart and your head ask those terrible questions, and let your heart know the truth of our hope that, in

spirit, *your loved one, like Jesus, is risen from earth's life to new life.*

It is true and well you know it: *she is not here;*
it is also true: *she is risen.*
Believe what God is telling you in your heart :
that love does last and the love you have shared is not lost.
Love is temporarily out of sight: your love is risen with
   God,
and you will one day rise in that love,
united with all in Christ.


# Day 9

## Scripture Reading

Jesus said:
"In all truth I tell you,
unless a wheat grain falls into the earth and dies,
it remains only a single grain;
but if it dies
it yields a rich harvest.
Anyone who loves his life loses it;
anyone who hates his life in this world
will keep it for eternal life".

*(John 12: 24-25)*


## Reflection
Life's little deaths point the way to little resurrections:
failure, even if devastating,  can lead to strength,
love which is questioned, can become stronger in its trust,
times when all seems dust or ashes, can give way to light.

Is it not the same with death?
Some of life's silver linings have been lost
– a love which was the mainstay of a family,
or a friendship which supported a life,
or a child who brought joy and love –
their death is their birth to Christ's new life,
and can be a source of new life for those left behind.

The final dust or ashes is the beginning of new life
– unseen, unfelt, unheard on earth;
the promise of new visions for the eye,
new songs for the ear,
new love for the heart,
glimpsed on earth, forever in eternity.

As Jesus enjoys eternity, so shall we, in his mercy.

## DAY 10

**Scripture Reading**

Writing to the Corinthian Christians St Paul said: The tradition I handed on to you in the first place, a tradition which I had myself received, was that Christ died for our sins, and that he was buried; and that on the third day, he was raised to life.

*(1 Corinthians 15: 3-4)*

**Reflection**
We do not think of death without mention of resurrection: this is the Christian way. When we think of life, we think of life here on earth and in eternity. When we remember love,

we remember love alive once on earth and now in eternity. When we recall friendship, we recall what was alive once in mortal life, and forever in eternal life. Our family is not only for this life: we will be reunited in reconciliation, understanding and love in heaven. Nothing good in us will be lost in death; our eyes are closed to its new life just for a while. As Jesus rose on the third day, we too will have third days, days when our eyes will be opened to new beauty, to new love and to new joy. This is our faith and this is our hope. May we live in the love of God which increases this faith and enlivens our hope.

## DAY 11

**Scripture Reading**

Writing to the Corinthian Christians St Paul said: If Christ is proclaimed as raised from the dead, how can some of you be saying that there is no resurrection of dead? If there is no resurrection of the dead, then Christ cannot have been raised either, and if Christ has not been raised, then our preaching is without substance, and so is your faith.

*(1 Corinthians 15: 12-13)*

**Reflection**
Why hope?
Why hope for life when all I sense is death?
Why hope for joy when all I recall are regrets?
Why hope when all I ask is why?

Hope that life follows death
as sunrise follows sunset,
and that the darkness in between will be bathed in light.

Hope that we will enjoy eternal youth,
for death can make us old with burdens,
and we hope to be light again,
as Jesus was youthful and light
in his risen life.

Our hope is green in the new life of Christ,
as 'the sadness of death gives way
to the bright promise of immortality'.


# Day 12

## Scripture Reading

When we were baptised into Christ Jesus, we were baptised
into his death. So by our baptism into his death we were
buried with him, so that as Christ was raised from the dead
by the Father's glorious power, we too should begin living a
new life. If we have been joined to him by dying a death like
his, so we shall be by a resurrection like his.

*(Romans 6:3-5)*

## Reflection

We look for reminders of life at the time of death. We look
for signs of life when all around feels dead and our heart is
dying, for signs of warmth in the cold face of death, and for
signs that life can continue when it seems to be ending.
Maybe that is why the presence of children eases the grief of
death: they remind us that life is continuing. In all these
ways, and many others, the presence of Christ is near to us.
The risen Christ is alive in the exuberance of our children,
is warm in the friendships that support us, and is eternal

when we think everything will pass.

Our hope as Christians in the face of death is rooted in the resurrection of Jesus. As he now lives with his Father, we too will live with God. The death of our loved one reminds us of our own death. Indeed, Jesus has gone ahead of us to prepare a place for us. In life, in death, O Lord, abide with me.

## Day 13

**Scripture Reading**

Jesus said:
"Anyone who does eat my flesh and drink my blood
has eternal life,
and I shall raise that person up on the last day.
This is the bread which has come down from heaven, anyone who eats this bread will live forever."

*(John 6:54, 58a,c)*

**Reflection**
From Jesus a promise,
a promise to us all:
if we share his body and blood in this life,
we shall share eternal life with him in the next.
Our loved ones have shared his body and blood in this life,
and now, in the spirit, they share eternal life with the Lord,
just as he promised.

The bread he gives is a bread broken in death:
He is the one who knows what it is like

to miss a father,
to comfort a bereaved mother,
to mourn a close friend,
to be with  friends whose brother has died,
and to face with courage one's own death.

With these ingredients he bakes the bread of life;
and these are the ingredients of our life too.
We need the nourishment of the bread of heaven
to feed us on the way to heaven.
In eating it, we are fed with courage and hope and love.
In being fed with God's bread together
we share faith with each other;
in sharing God's bread
we gather our hopes into the life of Jesus,
and in gathering around the bread of life
we celebrate the risen Christ.
And the same risen Lord
promises to each of us
life forever.


# Day 14

### Scripture Reading

Jesus said to Martha,
"I am the resurrection.
Anyone who believes in me,  even though that person dies,
    will live,
and whoever lives and believes in me
will never die.
Do you believe this?"

*(John 11:25-26)*

## Reflection

The question to Martha at her brother's death
is the question asked of each of us:
Do you believe that Jesus is the resurrection?
Do you really believe in life that never ends?
In the face of death can you still hope?

We believe because of the belief of Jesus.
In sadness we know he believed when his friend had died,
in confusion we know he believed when he asked that death
    pass him by,
in pain we know that he believed when he thought he was
    forsaken.

We believe because of the presence of Jesus
in those who offer us friendship at a hard time,
in the word of the Church at Mass and prayer,
in the glimpse of God in the new life of a tree in bud,
and in many countless ways
we get a glimpse,
sometimes just enough to keep going,
that there are mysteries of life
as yet unseen, unfelt and unheard.

We believe because of Jesus,
because he rose from death,
and because we know him to be alive
in the love surrounding us.

# WEEK 3

# IN THE FACE OF DEATH
# WE REMEMBER AND
# CELEBRATE OUR COMMUNION

## INTRODUCTION TO THE WEEK

When we lose a loved one through death, we spend much time thinking of them. As we do so they may often seem to be so present with us that we expect to be able to touch them; we may even talk to them. It is so important to remember our loved ones that the Church sets aside a whole month, November, as a special time for remembering all the souls of the faithful departed. Our ability to remember is one of the things that makes us human and also one of the things at the heart of our faith.

To remember is to allow our loved ones to continue to live in our lives. It is to put back together what has been dismembered, what has been taken away, what has become disconnected from the present. Memory reconnects the present with the past, putting us in touch with our roots and our human identity. Memory sustains us in the present and enables us to come through difficult times. If we forget our dead, our friends, our parents, our husband, our wife, our children, our dear ones, we cut ourselves off from the wellsprings of our life and the sources of our identity. We are who we are because of the influence on us of our loved ones who have died.

The activity of remembering is at the core of our religious faith. The centrepiece of Christianity is a remembering of the saving death and resurrection of Christ, that is, a recalling of his journey from historical existence into eternal glory. The Christian community remembers the death and resurrection of Christ in and through the Eucharist. We remember our dead in a very special way in the Mass, because the Eucharist re-enacts the Passover of Christ and the Passover of all the faithful departed who have followed in his footsteps into eternal life. Thus, when we gather to celebrate the Eucharist we celebrate the unity of the living and the dead in Christ. We remember those who have passed away, not only as dead but as living in Christ, not only as past but as present in the Body of Christ, not only as isolated but as living in communion with the saints, not only as removed from us but as with us in a new way in our journey to eternity.

> I believe in the Holy Spirit,
> the holy catholic Church,
> the communion of saints,
> the forgiveness of sins,
> the resurrection of the body,
> and life everlasting. Amen.

*(Apostles Creed)*

## Opening prayer

In the name of the Father and of the Son,
and of the Holy Spirit.
Amen.

Lord Jesus, you are the promise and image of what we shall be:
> Lord have mercy.

*(OCFI 95)*

Lord Jesus, you are the Bread of Life,
who nourished N. at the table of the Eucharist during
his/her earthly life. Welcome him/her at the table of God's
children in heaven.

Christ have mercy.

*(OCFI 218 adapted)*

Lord Jesus, remember those who have died alone. May they
be with you this day in paradise.

Lord have mercy.

**Reading and Reflection**
*(see separate days)*

**Concluding Prayer**
Let us pray as Jesus taught us:
        Our Father...

Father of mercies and God of all consolation,
Let N. pass unharmed through the gates of death
to dwell with the blessed in light.
Take him/her into your safekeeping
and on the great day of judgment
raise him/her up with all the saints
to inherit your kingdom for ever.

*(OCFI 58 adapted)*

By dying your Son has destroyed our death,
and by rising has restored our life.
When our own earthly course is run,
may he reunite us with those we love,
when every tear will be wiped away.

*(OCFI 58 adapted)*

May the God of all consolation
bring us comfort and peace,
in the name of the Father, and of the Son,
and of the Holy Spirit.
Amen.

(OCFI 241B)

## Day 15

### Scripture Reading

Be angry, but sin not;
commune with your own hearts on
your beds, and be silent.

(Psalm 4:4)

### Reflection

As we think of the death of our loved one traces of anger
may rise within us: anger with the hospital or the undertak-
ers, anger about the way the funeral went, even anger with
God for allowing our loved one to die, or for not hearing
our prayers.

Anger with God is perfectly understandable under the circumstances of pain arising from the loss of our loved one.
Anger with God is quite common in the Bible: we find it in
the Psalms, in the Book of Job, and even in the life of Jesus.
Passages such as today's scripture text can help us to
express our anger before God. Only when we have
acknowledged such anger are we really free to praise and
thank God for the gifts of life and health that our loved one
shared at other times before death. Our lament can give way
to praise, our anger to wonder, our resentment to accep-

tance of God's incomprehensible will. Prayer, especially at times of bereavement, knows many moods. We should not be afraid to own these many moods in our acts of loving and trusting in God.

## Day 16

### Scripture Reading

For I am certain of this: neither death nor life, nor angels, nor principalities, nothing already in existence and nothing still to come, nor any power, nor the heights nor the depths, nor any created thing whatever, will be able to come between us and the love of God, known to us in Christ Jesus our Lord.

*(Romans 8:38-39)*

### Reflection

As we seek to move from anger to hope, it is helpful to reflect that life itself is a gift and grace from God who created each of us out of love through our parents. We have not earned this gift in any way, and, if we are honest with ourselves, we know that we have often squandered the gift in different ways. Yet we continue to be sustained in existence by a loving God who upholds both the life of the universe itself and the life of each one of us. It is this same God who greets us in death and transforms us into a New Creation. This God who created the loved one whom we have lost in death is the God who will raise him or her into the fullness of life.

We hope in this future for our dead family and friends, and for ourselves, because of our knowledge that the love of

God brought us into being in the first place. The love of God is a steadfast love. Thus eternal life offered in the resurrection from the dead is not some kind of addition to human nature, but rather the fulfilment of the one gift of life itself already given by God at the moment of creation.

## DAY 17

### Scripture Reading

Jesus said:
"I am the living bread which has come down from heaven. Anyone who eats this bread
will live for ever; and the bread that I shall give
is my flesh, for the life of the world. Anyone who does eat my flesh and drink my blood has eternal life."

*(John 6: 51, 54)*

### Reflection
During their lives our loved ones shared in the Eucharist, communing in the flesh and blood of the Lord. Our hope is therefore that they share in the promise of Jesus that anyone who eats this bread will live for ever. In trying to cope with death, especially its darkness and coldness, it is good to remember the Eucharist. The celebration in which we share, in which our loved one shared, is a memorial of Christ's death and resurrection and the promise of our future life.

In his death Jesus was one with the whole of humanity, experiencing pain, fear, aloneness and absurdity. Yet his death was uniquely sacrificial and salvific. In death he represented all human beings in their struggle with death. The darkness surrounding his death is overcome by the light of his resurrection. The resurrection of Jesus does not remove the darkness of death – but it does mean that death does not have the final word, that death is not the end, that death is not annihilation. Resurrection is the other side of death, the outcome of that final journey that we must all make alone. Jesus is the one who has broken through the bonds of death and passed over into eternal glory. In the Eucharist we are united with this Risen Jesus.

Through Christ and in Christ, the riddles of sorrow and death grow meaningful (*Gaudium et spes*, 22). The death and resurrection of Jesus assure us that those who die in Christ will live for ever in communion with God. Our loved ones will be raised up into newness of life and one day we too will be reunited with them in Christ, the living bread which has come down from heaven.

## DAY 18

### Scripture Reading

When the two disciples drew near to the village to which they were going, Jesus made as if to go on; but they pressed him to stay with them saying, "It is nearly evening, and the day is almost over." So he went in to stay with them. Now while he was with them at table, he took the bread and said the blessing; then he broke it and handed it to them. And their eyes were opened and they recognised him; but he had vanished from their sight.

*(Luke 24:28-31)*

### Reflection
In their intense grief for their loved one who had been cruci-fied the two disciples were unable to recognise his continu-

ing presence with them until they arrived at an inn. In the familiar actions of taking, blessing, breaking and sharing bread they finally recognised the real, continuing presence of the Lord in their midst. The Eucharist connects this world with the transcendent world, the past with the present, the finite with the infinite. Once the two disciples had recognised the presence of the Lord with them in the Eucharist they no longer had need of his continuing physical presence. Through the Eucharist they were in communion with their loved one who had died and who had been raised to newness of life.

There is an intimate union between God, the saints and ourselves. Together we form a communion. Death is a journey to union with a passionate God, a surrender to his loving embrace. Our hope is that our loved one who has died has joined the community of the saints and now sees clearly that which we can only partly glimpse during this life. One day we too will join them. Together we form the one Body of Christ.

When we gather to celebrate the Eucharist we do so in communion with the heavenly assembly, joining together in one act of worship. There is but the thin veil of death between us.

## DAY 19

### Scripture Reading

I saw that there was a huge number, impossible for anyone to count, of people from every nation, race, tribe, and language; they were standing in front of the throne and in front of the Lamb, dressed in white robes and holding palms in their hands. And all the angels who were standing in a circle round the throne, surrounding the elders, prostrated themselves before the throne, and touched the ground with their foreheads, worshipping God.

*(Revelation 7: 9,11)*

### Reflection

Death diminishes all of us since a part of us also dies with the person we love who has passed away. We need to recognise this loss in ourselves, as well as the loss of our loved one, in death. Not to do so is to pretend that nothing has happened when, in fact, something very serious has happened and our lives can never return to their former ways. If our own brokenness is to be healed we must begin to accept the reality of our loved one's death. This does not mean we should forget our dead, nor does it mean that we are to seem indifferent. Rather, acceptance comes from recognising that ultimately death is part of God's larger plan, a plan that we cannot fully understand.

A glimpse of this larger plan is given to us in the above scripture passage. Our hope is that our loved ones are now joined to the Communion of Saints, and that they share in the heavenly banquet, the new feast of life. We can join them in their act of worship if, in prayer, we begin to let go of the person who has died, and to pray our goodbyes, by yielding our loved one up to the all-embracing love of God.

> May the angels lead you into paradise;
> may the martyrs come to welcome you
> and take you to the holy city,
> the new and eternal Jerusalem.

*(OCFI 185C)*

# Day 20

## Scripture Reading

The (younger) son said, "Father, I have sinned against heaven and against you. I no longer deserve to be called your son." But the father said to his servants, "Quick! Bring out the best robe and put it on him; put a ring on his finger and sandals on his feet. Bring the calf we have been fattening, and kill it; we will celebrate by having a feast, because this son of mine was dead and has come back to life."

*(Luke 15: 21-24)*

## Reflection

One of the obstacles we face during the period following the death of our loved one may be our image of God. Many people, like the young son in the parable extract above, have a fear-filled image of God as one who wishes to punish us for every single little defect in our lives. Since each of us has many defects, we often think with the Psalmist that *if you, O Lord, should mark our guilt, Lord, who would survive? (Psalm 130)*. We may therefore be reluctant to number our loved one among the ranks of the blessed in heaven.

Jesus' parable presents us with another image of God, a God of compassion, a God of love and forgiveness. The younger son, upon his return to the family home, is accepted fully by the Father whom he has grievously wronged. Because of the compassion of the Father the one who was dead is brought back to life, and joins in the feast of celebration.

By the infinite mercy of God, our loved one who has died will be brought back to life and will share with all the saints in the heavenly banquet. *For, with the Lord, there is mercy and fullness of redemption (Psalm 130).*

# Day 21

## Scripture Reading

Blessed be God the Father of our Lord Jesus Christ, who in his great mercy has given us a new birth into a living hope through the resurrection of Jesus Christ from the dead and into a heritage that can never be spoilt or soiled and never fade away. It is reserved in heaven for you.

*(1 Peter 1: 3-4)*

## Reflection

The first letter of Peter talks of us being born into a new hope through the resurrection of Jesus from the dead. It may well be that the death of our loved one has forced us to think seriously for the first time about the importance of hope. The virtue of hope, in contrast to faith and love, is neglected by many. Yet an active hope is essential to living a full Christian life. We all have hopes for this life, but underlying these little hopes there is our absolute hope in the future grounded in our faith in the existence of a caring and provident God, and our experience of his love.

The resurrection of Jesus gives us a hope that can never be spoilt or soiled or fade away; our loved ones and we ourselves will share new life in Christ in communion with the saints. With such hope in our hearts, we can slowly pick up the pieces of our lives after the trauma of the death of someone we love. We can have a firm hope in their well-being and happiness and in our own future following their loss. By his life, death and resurrection Jesus has *blazed a trail, and if we follow it, life and death are made holy and take on a new meaning* (*Gaudium et spes, 22*).

# WEEK 4

# IN THE FACE OF DEATH WE CONFIDENTLY HOPE THAT OUR LOVED ONES REST IN PEACE

## INTRODUCTION TO THE WEEK

Blessed are those who have died in the Lord;
let them rest from their labours for their good deeds go with them.

*(OCFI 69)*

Slowly, imperceptibly, we are struggling to come to terms with the reality of our loved one's death, and the depth of our loss. While the pain remains, the numbness and tiredness may just be beginning to lift a little. Through faith we may accept that God has called our loved one, but it is harder to accept that our loved one has left us.

Our hope is that our loved one rests in peace. This is the source of our consolation, this is what can give light to our darkness. We pray that God will say to our loved one "I have called you by your name, you are mine, you are precious to me, and I love you". This divine promise reassures us and insists that death is not the end. By this love Jesus can promise us that we who mourn will be comforted. This is the love of God which we so often experience through the understanding and support of others, a love that enables us to survive the unsurviveable.

45

As he approached his own death, Jesus promised the one who was dying alongside him: "Today you will be with me in paradise". It is our sure hope that our loved one will also rest in paradise with Christ, and that one day we too will share his peace.

**Opening prayer**

In the name of the Father and of the Son,
and of the Holy Spirit.
Amen.

Lord Jesus, you are the Son of God who has destroyed sin and death:
  Lord, have mercy.

(OCFI 95 adapted)

Lord Jesus, you are the gentle Shepherd who brings rest and peace to N. for ever:
  Christ, have mercy.

(OCFI 95)

Lord Jesus, you also give refreshment, rest and peace to all whose faith is known to you alone.
  Lord, have mercy.

(OCFI 177A adapted)

**Reading and Reflection**
*(see separate days)*

**Concluding Prayer**

We pray as Jesus taught us:

Our Father...

Lord of all gentleness,
surround us with your care
and comfort us in our sorrow
for we grieve at the loss of N.
Welcome him/her into the life of heaven
and call us one day
to be united with him/her
and share for ever the joy of your kingdom.
(*OCFI 240A adapted*)

May the God of all consolation
bring us comfort and peace,
in the name of the Father, and of the Son,
and of the Holy Spirit.
Amen.

(*OCFI 241B*)

(See also *The Song of Farewell*, p. 65)

## Day 22

### Scripture Reading

Jesus raised his eyes to heaven and said:
Father,
I want those you have given me
to be with me where I am,
so that they may always see my glory
which you have given me
because you loved me
before the foundation of the world.

(*John 17:1a, 24*)

## Reflection

These words were spoken by Jesus during the last meal he shared with his family of disciples. At a time of coming separation he talked of a love that had existed since before time itself, a love that would continue in the face of separation and which would ensure that his disciples would join with him in his risen, glorified state.

Jesus was not only talking to those who shared his table that night, he was also speaking to us and to our loved ones who have followed him along the way. His prayer on that night before his death was for us all. From this promise of the Lord we find hope and consolation as we grieve during this time of painful separation.

## Day 23

### Scripture Reading

God takes no pleasure in the extinction of the living.
To be – for this he created all.
The souls of the upright are in the hands of God,
and no torment can touch them.
They are at peace.

*(Wisdom 1:13b-14, 3:1, 3b)*

### Reflection

God, the source of life, calls each of us to fullness of life, not to extinction. He has created each of us for life, not for death. There is a continuity between this life and eternal life. Death is but the gateway between the two. God is the God of the living, not of the dead; Jesus is the resurrection, whoever believes in him, lives in him, and can never die.

Our loved one may have died slowly and painfully, or suddenly and unexpectedly, or they may have slipped away quietly and gently. Whatever way death came, we know that no pain or hurt of mind or body can touch them now. We are grateful that no fear or worry can trouble them. In the darkness of our pain and loss, a light of consolation shines in the promise that our loved one will receive the gift of peace, a peace that this world cannot give.

# Day 24

**Scripture Reading**

When the tent that houses us on earth is folded up,
there is a house for us from God,
not made by human hands but everlasting,
in the heavens.

*(2 Corinthians 5:1)*

**Reflection**

St Paul was a tent-maker by trade so he draws upon personal experience when he talks of death in terms of a nomad folding up a tent so that he can move on on his journey to live in another place. Some tents are made of sturdier materials than others, but no matter how strong, eventually all of them begin to show signs of wear, and eventually they are folded up for the last time, their usefulness exhausted.

Death is a kind of folding-up of the tent that houses us here on earth. The tent of our body does indeed wear out, it lasts for only a limited time. It has served us well on our journey through life, but like any tent it is not a permanent dwelling.

Our hope comes from the promise that when the tent of this life is folded up we will not be left without shelter. The faded tent will be replaced by a more sturdy, lasting structure, a house in the heavens, a house built not by human hands, but which comes from God. In death the place of our dwelling is transformed from that which is temporary to that which is permanent, from that which is weak to that which is strong, from that which is human-made to that which is God-made. And to each of us Jesus has promised that in his Father's house there are many places to live.

## DAY 25

### Scripture Reading

Jesus said:
Do not let your hearts be troubled.
You trust in God, trust also in me.
In my Father's house there are many places to live in; otherwise I would have told you.
I am going to prepare a place for you.
I shall return to take you to myself,
so that you may be with me
where I am.

*(John 14: 1-3)*

### Reflection
This message of understanding and compassion is repeated time and time again in the Scriptures – telling us that no matter what happens God is always with us; telling us that Jesus understands our feelings of insecurity, our need for acceptance, and our need to be sure that our loved one will be welcome in his Father's house.

God is a merciful and loving parent. He wants all his children to be with him, from every race, every nationality, every creed. No matter how great our feelings of unworthiness, God still longs to welcome us to his eternal home. Jesus came to call sinners to repentance, he went out to the highways and the byways to invite all to the wedding feast, he searched for the lost sheep as well as those that never strayed. We should not worry about the love of God for our loved one. We should trust in God and in Jesus, whose deep desire was for us to be with him in the presence of his Father.

## Day 26

### Scripture Reading

Peter said, "I now really understand", he said, "that God has no favourites, but that anybody of any nationality who fears him and does what is right is acceptable to him".

*(Acts 10: 34-35)*

### Reflection

How quick we are to limit God, to define who is acceptable to him and who is not, to specify who is saved and who is not. A heaven limited to the few is not the kingdom that Jesus preached. He came so that all would be saved. He is a shepherd who wishes that not one sheep should be lost. He welcomed and healed all who came to him, be they prostitutes such as Mary of Magdala, or collaborators with the forces of occupation such as Zacchaeus the corrupt tax-collector, or members of the occupying Roman army themselves, or a thief dying on a cross next to him.

We are painfully aware of our own shortcomings, and we know that our loved ones had their own shortcomings too.

We should not worry about these. It is not up to us to measure the depth of their faith, or to judge their actions. We will leave that up to God in his infinite mercy and love.

## DAY 27

### Scripture Reading

> As a deer yearns
> for running streams,
> so I yearn
> for you, my God.
>
> I thirst for God,
> the living God:
> when shall I go to see
> the face of God?

*(Psalm 42: 1-2)*

### Reflection

At the time of our loved one's death, and during the days that followed it, there were many neighbours, relatives and friends to share our grief. They are still supporting us, but we know that they have other commitments, other responsibilities. As we face each day, having to rely more and more on ourselves, there is an emptiness within us, yearning to be filled. Paradoxically, this very emptiness can help us understand the death of our loved one.

We yearn for love and intimacy, we long to be close to the one we love. Such human yearning is part of the yearning of the inner core of each of us to be close to God, to experience a perfect and lasting love, a love that transforms and heals. God is love itself. Only when we are embraced fully by the love of God can we be fully complete and at peace. Through faith we know that our loved one has fulfilled the deepest yearning of the human heart, and now rests in God, looking upon God's face as a newborn infant at the breast looks upon the face of its mother. Our deep love for our beloved invites us to surrender them into the fathomless love of God. Through such surrender we too will experience peace.

## Day 28

### Scripture Reading

> I hear my love.
> See how he comes
> leaping on the mountains,
> bounding over the hills.
>
> See where he stands
> behind our wall.
> He looks in at the window,
> he peers through the opening.
>
> My love lifts up his voice,
> he says to me,
> "Come then, my beloved,
> my lovely one, come."

*(Song of Songs 2:8, 9b-10)*

### Reflection
How deeply we miss our loved one, their touch, their voice, their smile, their presence. How we long not just to see them again, but to be seen by them; not only to touch them, but to be touched by them. We experience the pain of their loss with each of our senses.

Our last images of our loved one may be pain-filled. It is hard to watch the gradual deterioration of the body of one we love, hard to accept the change in personality that serious illness often brings, and just as hard to grasp the reality of any form of sudden death. For a while such painful images may dominate our memories, blocking out all other images. But we have other memories and images of our loved one as beautiful and life-filled. We may have been trying to put such thoughts and images aside until we feel better able to cope with them. We should let them come back into our mind's eye.

The above verses of Scripture may help us to acknowledge such other images. At first glance the verses speak of the beauty of human love, of relationships that we may have shared. At a deeper level they speak of God as being a lover, a lover actively courting his beloved. His beloved and our loved one are the same. At the moment of death our loved one has passed from our loving embrace into the embrace of a loving God, a God who looks upon the one we have loved and sees them as beautiful, and who leads them by the hand to a new life.

# WEEK 5

# LOVE ONE ANOTHER
# AS I HAVE LOVED YOU

## INTRODUCTION TO THE WEEK

The angels said: "Jesus has risen from the dead and now he is going ahead of you to Galilee; that is where you will see him".

*(Matthew 28:7)*

There is a time to remain at the grave. Jesus was entombed for three days after which he was released from the tomb. Our faith is that Jesus rose from the dead, and our hope is that that our loved ones who have died will share his new life in spirit. In the midst of our mourning we ask ourselves "are we to be the only ones who remain trapped by the sorrow of death in the tomb of our grief?" There will be a time when we turn our gaze from the grave towards the living. Our faith in Christ will free us to do so.

Jesus rose and goes before us into Galilee, the place where he grew up, the place where he worked as a carpenter, the place where he preached, the place where he healed. In time we will follow him away from the tomb and share his message of love. Jesus invites us to find new life in our sorrow by living and loving as he did. In this way we will remember and be united with our loved one who has gone before us.

## Opening prayer

In the name of the Father and of the Son,
and of the Holy Spirit.
Amen.

Crucified Lord, forsaken in death, raised in glory:
Lord, have mercy.

*(OCFI 95)*

Gentle Shepherd, into your hands we commit our
beloved N.
Christ, have mercy.

Lord, many people die by violence, war and famine each
day. Show your mercy to those who suffer unjustly these
sins against your love, and gather them to your eternal
kingdom of peace.
Lord, have mercy.

*(OCFI 177A adapted)*

## Reading and Reflection
*(see separate days)*

## Concluding Prayer

We pray as Jesus taught us:

Our Father...

Loving Lord, from whom all life proceeds,
look with favour upon N., our beloved.
Deliver his/her soul from death,

number him/her among your saints,
and clothe him/her with the robe of salvation
to enjoy forever the delights of your kingdom.

*(OCFI 224B adapted)*

Lord, while we await the day of your coming,
make us an instrument of your peace:
where there is hatred, let us sow love,
where there is injury, forgiveness;
where there is doubt, faith;
where there is despair, hope;
where there is darkness, light;
where there is sadness, joy.
And when our earthly journey is ended,
lead us rejoicing into your kingdom,
where you live for ever and ever.
Amen.

*(traditional and OCFI 332)*

May the God of all consolation
bring us comfort and peace,
in the name of the Father, and of the Son,
and of the Holy Spirit.
Amen.

*(OCFI 241B)*

# DAY 29

### Scripture Reading

As he neared death Tobit summoned his son Tobias and
told him: "My child, be faithful to the Lord all your days.
Never turn your face from the poor and God will never turn
his from you. Do not keep back until next day the wages of
those who work for you; pay them at once. Do to no one

what you would not want done to you. Give your bread to those who are hungry, and your clothes to those who lack clothing. Bless the Lord God in everything; beg him to guide your ways and bring your paths and purposes to their end."

*(Tobit 4:3, 5a, 7b, 14a, 15a, 16a, 19a)*

### Reflection
The challenge to pick up the shattered pieces of our lives. We may not want to do so; we may not now have the energy to do so, but in time we will do so. It is true that we will never really be the same again; the burden of sorrow can never be fully removed, although we will learn to carry it. To deny our brokenness would be to deny the depth of the love we shared with our loved one who has died.

If we remain with our eyes fixed only on the past we will be lost in our brokenness. Paradoxically, our greatest strength to face the present and the future can come from our very brokenness. Because we experience sorrow, we can be sensitive to the sorrow of others; because we mourn, we can comfort those who mourn; our hurt opens us to the hurt of others.

It is in this very openness that we find the presence of the loved one whom we have lost. Like Tobit our loved one cherished that which is good. What he or she stood for can continue to live through us; the good that he or she did can still bear fruit on this earth through our lives.

# DAY 30

## Scripture Reading

Jesus said:
"Little children,
I shall be with you only a little longer.
I give you a new commandment:
love one another;
you must love one another
just as I have loved you."

*(John 13: 33a, 34)*

## Reflection

The parting words of one we love are words that we will remember all our lives. On the night before he died, Jesus' parting words to his friends were about love. While he was with them he sustained them through his love. Now they are to be sustained by loving as he loved.

When one who loves us dies, the very core of our being seems to die with them. We may feel that we have lost the ability to love and to care. If this is really the case then our body becomes a living tomb for our spirits. It is the power of love that enables us to rise from among the dead ourselves and to keep on living.

St Paul reminds us that love never ends; it is always ready to trust, to hope, and to endure whatever comes. The love that our loved one gave us during his or her time with us can never be destroyed, can never die. It can still sustain us after his or her death. If, in our brokenness, we can find the courage to share love with others who are broken then we will continue to be sustained by the love of those who have died. The love that Jesus shared was a love unto death and a love that survived death. His love was a total giving of himself. He invites us to love in the same way.

## DAY 31
*(or the day of the Month's Mind Mass)*

### Scripture Reading

The two disciples returned from Emmaus to Jerusalem. There they found the Eleven (apostles) and told their story of what had happened on the road and how they had recognised Jesus at the breaking of the bread. They were still talking about all this when he himself stood among them and said to them "Peace be with you".
*(Luke 24:33-37)*

### Reflection

Our journey in the past month has been so like that of the two disciples. Confused and hurt after the death of Jesus they escaped from the everyday world of Jerusalem seeking to hide from that which they could not face. Their deep brokenness prevented them from recognising the presence of the Lord with them. Only when they began to open themselves to a fellow traveller did they begin to experience the presence of the loved one they longed to see. Arriving at an inn they finally recognised the presence of Christ in their midst in Eucharistic bread, blessed, broken and shared. It is right that we too should celebrate the Eucharist with those we love to remember our loved one who has died.

In returning to Jerusalem the two disciples faced what, in their sorrow, they could not face. In the very place they expected to find emptiness they experienced, as they shared deeply with others who mourned, the presence of their loved one. There is a time in our lives also to return to Jerusalem, confident that love cannot be destroyed by death, and slowly opening ourselves to the needs of others.

"Peace be with you", is the greeting of the Risen, glorified Christ. It is his special greeting to those who mourn, the greeting of one who himself suffered an agonising death, and who, at times, felt that even God had deserted him. Only those who have been broken, who have experienced pain and sorrow, whose hearts have been downcast, can really understand the meaning of this greeting. May you too experience the peace of the Risen Lord in your life as you strive to share his love.

> May the Lord support us all day long,
> 'til the shades lengthen, and the
> evening comes,
> and the busy world is
> hushed,
> and the fever of life is over,
> and our work is done.
> Then in His
> mercy may He give us a safe lodging,
> and a holy rest,
> and peace at last.
>
> (*Cardinal Newman*)

PART TWO

# PRAYERS FOR THOSE
# WHO MOURN

# POPULAR PRAYERS FOR THOSE WHO HAVE DIED

Eternal rest grant unto him/her, O Lord.
And let perpetual light shine upon him/her.
May he/she rest in peace.
Amen.

May his/her soul and the souls of all the faithful departed,
through the mercy of God, rest in peace.
Amen.

## SONG OF FAREWELL

Saints of God, come to his/her aid!
Hasten to meet him/her, angels of the Lord!

Receive his/her soul
and present him/her to God the Most High.

May Christ, who called you, take you to himself:
may angels lead you to the bosom of Abraham.

Receive his/her soul
and present him/her to God the Most High.

Eternal rest grant unto him/her, O Lord.
And let perpetual light shine upon him/her.

Receive his/her soul
and present him/her to God the Most High.

(*OCFI 183*)

## SOME SHORT PRAYERS

N. (*name of the deceased*),
may the Lord bless you and keep you.
May he let his face shine on you
and be gracious to you.
May the Lord show you his face,
and bring you peace.

(*Numbers 6:23*)

May Christ now enfold you in his love
and bring you to eternal life.
We will pray for you, N.
(*name of the deceased*).
May you pray for us.
May God and Mary be with you.

(*OCFI 111*)

Lord,
into your hands we commit N.
(*name of deceased*),
our loved one.

Father,
Remember those who have died in the peace of Christ
and all the dead whose faith is known to you alone.

(*Eucharistic Prayer IV*)

# PRAYERS FOR FAMILY MEMBERS

### FAMILY PRAYER FOR A MEMBER WHO HAS DIED
*This prayer is written in the female form for a wife, mother, grandmother, daughter or sister. It is easily adapted to the male form for a husband, father, grandfather, son or brother.*

Lord, we gather as a family
in pain and sorrow,
to praise you for the life of N.
whom we love deeply,
and whom we now entrust to your tender care.

We thank you for the gift of her to us as a woman
      (as a wife
      as a mother
      as a grandmother,
      as a daughter
      as a sister
      as a friend).
N. was much loved by us, so near to us,
and now you have taken her to yourself,
to be united with you in love.

We thank you for the friendship that N. gave us,
for the love that she shared,
for the laughter that she caused,
for the peace that she brought.

We pray that nothing of N.'s life will be lost,
but will continue to be of benefit to others in this world.
We pray that all she held sacred
will continue to be respected by those of us who remain.

We pray that everything for which she worked,
will continue to bear fruit.

Finally, Lord, we pray that we who were loved by N. here
on earth may, through her death,
be drawn ever closer to each other
and one day we may be united with N.
together again in your heavenly home.

*(Adapted from Huub Oosterhuis, Your Word is Near)*

## UPON HEARING OF THE DEATH OF A LOVED ONE

Into your hands, O loving Father,
we humbly entrust our beloved N.
In this life you embraced him/her with your tender love;
deliver him/her now from every evil
and bid him/her enter eternal rest.
Welcome him/her into paradise,
where there will be no sorrow, no weeping nor pain,
but the fullness of peace and joy
with your Son and the Holy Spirit
for ever and ever.
Amen.

*(OCFI 68B adapted)*

## PARENTS' PRAYER ON THE DEATH OF A CHILD

### Scripture Verse

Length of days is not what makes age honourable,
nor number of years the true measure of life.
Having come to perfection so soon, he has lived long; his
soul being pleasing to the Lord.

*(Wisdom 4: 8,13, 14a)*

**Prayer**
Lord God,
source and destiny of our lives,
in your loving kindness
you gave us N.,
to grow in wisdom, age and grace.
Now you have called him/her to yourself.
We grieve over the loss of one so young
and struggle to understand your purpose.
Draw him/her to yourself
and give him/her full life in Christ.
Comfort us with the knowledge
that our child for whom we grieve
is now gathered in your loving care.

*(OCFI 252 A, B adapted)*


## PARENTS' PRAYER FOR A STILL-BORN CHILD

**Scripture Verse**

Before I formed you in the womb I knew you;
before you came to birth I consecrated you.

*(Jeremiah 1:5)*


*If your child has not been baptised, you may wish to name
him/her. The following prayer may help:*

God, our loving Father,
You have called each of us by name from all eternity.
Confident in your embracing love,
we name our child N.

N., may the Lord bless you and keep you,
may he let his face shine on you
and be gracious to you,
may he uncover his face to you
and bring you peace.

*(OCFI 249 adapted)*


God of kindness and compassion,
you created N. (our child) in your own image and likeness,
bestowing the gift of life,
a gift that is transformed,
but never taken away.
We entrust our child to your everlasting love.

We pray for ourselves, his/her parents.
You were with us in the time of happiness
when we conceived our child.
Be with us now in this time of sorrow,
and one day unite our family
in the peace and joy of your kingdom.

Amen.

*(OCFI 252C adapted)*

## GRACE BEFORE MEALS – FUNERAL TIME

### Scripture Verse

The two disciples pressed the Lord to stay with them. So he went in to stay with them. Now while he was with them at table, he took the bread and said the blessing; then he broke it and handed it to them. And their eyes were opened and they recognised him.

*(Luke 24: 29,30)*

### Prayer
Lord Jesus,
as we gather together around this table,
we see an empty place;
our eyes are downcast, our hearts are heavy.
We sense both the presence, and the absence of our
  beloved N.
who shared our table, our home and our lives.
Our hope is that he/she is now with you in your Father's
  house.
One day may we all be united once more
at the table of your heavenly banquet.
Bless all of us here gathered and the food that we share.
Open our eyes so that we may recognise you, our Risen
Lord, in each other,
and know your peace in our troubled lives.

## WHEN VISITING THE GRAVE OF A LOVED ONE

Lord Jesus Christ,
by your own three days in the tomb,
you hallowed the graves of all who believe in you

and so made the grave a sign of hope
that promises resurrection
even as it claims our mortal bodies.
Remember N., our beloved, who rests here,
may he/she sleep in peace
until you awaken him/her to glory,
for you are the resurrection and the life.

*(OCFI 220B adapted)*


## FOR ALL IN A GRAVEYARD

Remember, Lord, those who have died
and have gone before us marked with the sign of faith,
especially those for whom we now pray, N. and N.
May  these, and all who sleep in Christ,
find in your presence
light, happiness, and peace.

*(Eucharistic Prayer I)*

*or*

God of the living and the dead,
accept our prayers for those who have died in Christ
and are buried with him in the hope of rising again.
Since they were true to your name on earth,
let them praise you for ever in the joy of heaven.

*(OCFI 327)*


## ON AN ANNIVERSARY

Lord, there is a time for dying,
when you took N. to yourself,
and a time for re-birth,

when you restored him/her to life in the spirit
through your Son.

There is a time for tears,
when we grieved his/her loss,
and a time for hope,
when we were comforted by your promise of eternal life.

There is a time for healing,
when you sustained us through the support of others,
and a time for building,
when we slowly reshaped our shattered lives.

There is a time for searching,
as we seek to understand your ways,
and a time for losing,
when we finally surrender our loved one to your welcoming arms.

There is a time for remembering,
when we sense again the presence
of our loved one in our midst,
and a time for keeping silent,
as we stand before a mystery that we can
only dimly glimpse.

Indeed Lord, there is a season for everything,
a time for everything under heaven.

*(after Ecclesiastes 3: 1-8)*

## FOR THE SOULS IN PURGATORY

Father,
Remember all who have gone before us in the Lord;
may their suffering be lessened,
may their joy be increased,
may the light of glory shine on them
and may they rest in peace.
*(OCFI 222 adapted)*
Remember our brothers and sisters
who have gone to their rest
in the hope of rising again;
bring them and all the departed
into the light of your presence.

*(Eucharistic Prayer II)*

# PRAYERS DURING FUNERAL TIME

### While laying out the body

*The body may be sprinkled with holy water.*

The Lord God lives in his holy temple yet abides in our
   midst.
In baptism N. became God's temple
and the Spirit of God lived in him/her.
With reverence and love we prepare his/her
   mortal body
to await the resurrection of the dead.

*(OCFI 65C adapted)*

**When the coffin is to be sealed**

May Christ now enfold you in his love
and bring you to eternal life.

We will pray for you N.,
may you pray for us.

May God and Mary be with you.

*(OCFI 111)*

**When the remains are leaving the house**

May the love of God and the peace of the
Lord Jesus Christ
bless and console us
and gently wipe every tear from our eyes.

*(OCFI 69B)*

**With the remains in the church**

**Scripture verse**

Blessed be God
the Father of our Lord Jesus Christ,
who has blessed us
with all the spiritual blessings of heaven in Christ.
He chose us in Christ
before the world was made
to be holy and faultless
before him in love,
marking us out for himself beforehand,
to be his adopted children,
through Jesus Christ.

*(Ephesians 1: 3-5 adapted)*

**Prayer**

Father, the death of N.
forces us face the reality of our human condition
and the brevity of our lives on this earth.
For those who believe in your love
death is not the end,
and does not destroy the bonds
forged in our lives.
Bring the light of your Son's resurrection
to this time of pain and sorrow
as we/I pray for N. and for those who love him/her.

*(OCFI 89A adapted)*

*See also the Psalms and Devotions on pages 78-89.*

# PRAYERS FOR PARTICULAR SITUATIONS

FOR ONE WHO DIED AFTER A LONG ILLNESS

Lord God,
you are living water for our deepest thirst,
and manna in our desert dryness.
We praise you for the life of our beloved N.
and bless your mercy
in bringing his/her suffering to an end.
Raise him/her to new life
in the peace of Christ your Son.

FOR ONE WHO DIED SUDDENLY

Lord,
we are numbed by the sudden death
of our beloved N.
We suspected not the day nor the hour.

We pray that in your mercy and goodness,
you found him/her ready at the time of your coming,
and have led him/her into your presence.

FOR ONE WHO DIED BY VIOLENCE
Lord,
our sorrow at the death of N.
is made even stronger by the knowledge that
the life you gave him/her
was so tragically and suddenly ended.
Come swiftly to his/her aid,
forgive his/ her trespasses
and lead him/her to fullness of life in your kingdom.
Comfort us in our anguish
and remove any bitterness from our hearts.

*(OCFI 314.36 adapted)*

FOR ONE WHO DIED IN OLD AGE
Lord,
look kindly on our beloved N,
whose long life is now complete.
Give him/her a place in your kingdom,
and the fullness of your peace and joy.

*(OCFI 314 . 30, 31 adapted)*

FOR ONE WHO DIED BY SUICIDE
Lord,
in our great sorrow we trust in you
knowing that you are a just and loving God.
You hold dear all whom you have made
and spare all, for they are yours.
Look gently on our loved one, N.
Do not remember his/her sins

but look upon his/her sufferings of mind and body,
and grant him/her your rest and peace.

*(OCFI 314.33, 37, 38 adapted)*

FOR A RELIGIOUS
Loving Father,
our brother/sister N. spent his/her life following Jesus,
poor, chaste, and obedient.
Count him/her among all those holy men and women
who sing in your heavenly courts.

*(OCFI 177A adapted)*

FOR A PRIEST
Loving Father,
our brother N. shared in the ministerial priesthood
    of your Son,
leading his people in prayer and worship.
Bring him into your presence
where he will take his place for ever in the heavenly liturgy.

*(OCFI 177A adapted)*

# PSALMS

DE PROFUNDIS (PSALM 130)

Out of the depths I cry to you, O Lord,
Lord, hear my voice!
O let your ears be attentive
to the voice of my pleading.

If you, O Lord, should mark our guilt,
Lord, who could survive?

But with you is found forgiveness:
for this we revere you.

My soul is waiting for the Lord,
I count on his word.
My soul is longing for the Lord
more than watchman for daybreak.
Because with the Lord there is mercy
and fullness of redemption,
Israel indeed he will redeem
from all its iniquity.

*(OCFI 66)*

## THE LORD IS MY SHEPHERD (PSALM 22)

The Lord is my Shepherd:
there is nothing I shall want.
Fresh and green are the pastures
where he gives me repose.
Near restful waters he leads me,
to revive my drooping spirit.

He guides me along the right path;
he is true to his name.
If I should walk in the valley of darkness
no evil would I fear.
You are there with your crook and your staff;
with these you give me comfort.

You have prepared a banquet for me
in the sight of my foes.
My head you have anointed with oil;
my cup is overflowing.

Surely goodness and kindness shall follow me
all the days of my life.
In the Lord's own house shall I dwell
for ever and ever.

# DEVOTIONS

## THE ROSARY – WITH SHORT REFLECTIONS

*Each decade of the Rosary consists of reciting one Our Father, ten Hail Marys and one Glory Be while reflecting on a particular mystery from the Christian story. To assist this reflection short scriptural quotations are provided.*

### The Joyful Mysteries
In the face of death we recall the sources of life and recognise Jesus as our Lord and Saviour.

*The Annunciation*: The angel Gabriel said to Mary "The Lord is with you" (*Luke 1:28*). Mary was troubled by the turn her life was taking. It was hard to understand the will of God. Gabriel reassures her, God is with her, directing her life, sustaining, embracing.

*The Visitation*: After meeting Elizabeth, Mary prayed: "My spirit rejoices in God my Saviour" (*Luke 1:47*). At a time of confusion and hardship it is often through the support of others that we recognise God as the One who is active in our life.

*The Nativity:* The angel said to the shepherds "Do not be afraid, a Saviour has been born to you; he is Christ the

80

Lord" (*Luke 2:10,11*). During a time of loss we often lose our own self-identity, everything seems to have changed and we are afraid to face life without the company of our loved one. Trust in the Lord, he offers each of us his saving love.

*The Presentation of Jesus in the Temple:* Upon seeing Jesus, Simeon said: "Now, Master, you are letting your servant go in peace, as you promised; for my eyes have seen the salvation which you have made ready in the sight of the nations" (*Luke 2:29-31*). Peace is found in the recognition that death involves surrender, a letting-go of this life and the grasping of a fuller vision.

*The Finding of Jesus in the Temple*: Jesus said to his worried parents: "Why were you looking for me? Did you not know that I must be in my Father's house?" (*Luke 2:49-50*). All human relationships, especially those which are very close, must ultimately be prepared to free the individual for intimacy with God. Such intimacy is the deeper purpose of our lives.

**The Sorrowful Mysteries**
In the face of death we reflect on the passion and death of the Lord to ease our pain and to deepen our faith.

*The Agony in the Garden*: "During his life on earth, Jesus offered up prayer and entreaty, with loud cries and with tears, to the one who had the power to save him from death" (*Hebrews 5:7*). It is only human to fear the process of dying, but because of the obedience of Christ, we now have little reason to fear death itself.

*The Scourging at the Pillar*: "My strength is trickling away, my bones are all disjointed, my heart has turned to wax, melting inside me. My mouth is dry as earthenware, my tongue sticks to my jaw. You lay me down in the dust of death" (*Psalm 22:14-15*). How unbearable it is to stand powerless as those whom we love suffer pain and anguish. Jesus, Lamb of God, have mercy on us, Jesus, Lamb of God, grant us peace.

*The Crowning with Thorns*: "The governor's soldiers stripped Jesus and put a scarlet cloak round him, and having twisted some thorns into a crown they put this on his head and placed a reed in his right hand" (*Matthew 27:28-29*). To die is to be stripped of all dignity, to be clothed in pain, to be crowned with weakness, and to stand powerless before others. The paradox is that as this happens we become more and more like Christ .

*The Carrying of the Cross*: Jesus said "If anyone wants to be a follower of mine, let him renounce himself and take up his cross and follow me" (*Mark 8:34*). In the journey that is life we must carry the cross of pain and loss and sorrow. We do not journey alone, however, the Lord has journeyed ahead of us, and now accompanies us on our way.

*The Crucifixion*: "Jesus emptied himself, taking the form of a slave, becoming as human beings are; and being in every way like a human being, he was humbler yet, even to accepting death, death on a cross" (*Philippians 2:7-8*). In Christ, God the creator, source and sustainer of all life, accepted death, the death of a common criminal. In the absurdity of this mystery we find grace and salvation.

### Glorious Mysteries
In the face of death we look to the resurrection of the Lord, and to our share in his victory, as the source of our hope.

*The Resurrection*: "Why look among the dead for one who is alive?" (*Luke 24:5b*). A new dawn, a re-birth, a new creation, a new order. Lord, that I may see.

*The Ascension*: "Since you have been raised up to be with Christ, you must look for the things that are above, where Christ is, sitting at God's right hand" (*Colossians 3:1*). Death has no more power over those who have been restored to life in Christ. They will share his glory for ever.

*Pentecost:* "The fruit of the Spirit is love, joy, peace, patience, kindness, goodness, trustfulness, gentleness and self-control" (*Galatians 5:22*). Holy Spirit, Lord of Light, from the clear celestial height, thy pure beaming radiance give. Heal our wounds, our strength renew; on our dryness pour thy dew; wash the stains of guilt away. Give us comfort when we die; give us life with thee on high; give us joys that never end (*Sequence for Pentecost*).

*The Assumption of Mary*: "Christ has been raised from the dead, as the first-fruit of all who have fallen asleep" (*1 Corinthians 15:20*). The assumption of Mary to be with her Son in glory is a confirmation of the promise that we shall all share in his resurrection.

*The Coronation of Mary as Queen of Heaven:* "Now a great sign appeared in heaven: a woman, robed with the sun, standing on the moon, and on her head a crown of twelve stars" (*Revelation 12:1*). When we pray we are in communion with Mary, the saints and our loved ones, joined in one eternal act of praise and thanksgiving. Holy Mary, mother of God, pray for us sinners, now and at the hour of our death.

*After the last decade one of the following is said:*

Hail, holy Queen, Mother of mercy,
hail, our life, our sweetness, and our hope.
To you we cry, poor children of Eve:
to you we send up our sighs,
mourning and weeping in this vale of tears.
Turn, then, most gracious advocate,
your eyes of mercy towards us;
and after this our exile, show unto us
the blessed fruit of your womb, Jesus:
O clement, O loving, O sweet Virgin Mary.

Let us pray:
O God, whose only begotten Son, by his life, death and resurrection, has purchased for us the rewards of eternal life;
grant, we beseech you, that meditating on these mysteries of
the most holy Rosary of the Blessed Virgin Mary, we may
both initiate what they contain and obtain what they
promise, through the same Christ our Lord. Amen.

*or*

May the prayers of Mary, the Mother of God,
who stood by the cross as her Son was dying,
help us who mourn for N. (*name of the deceased*),
and accompany all of us in our time of need.

*(OCFI 226)*

## THE WAY OF THE CROSS

**Before each Station:**
We adore you, O Christ, and we bless you,
Because of your holy cross
you have redeemed the world.
**After each Station:**
Dying you destroyed our death,
Rising you restored our life,
Lord Jesus, come in glory.

1. Jesus is condemned to death
2. Jesus carries his cross
3. Jesus falls the first time
4. Jesus meets his mother
5. Simon of Cyrene helps Jesus to carry his cross
6. Veronica wipes the face of Jesus
7. Jesus falls the second time
8. Jesus meets the women of Jerusalem
9. Jesus falls the third time
10. Jesus is stripped of his garments
11. Jesus is nailed to the cross
12. Jesus dies on the cross
13. Jesus' body is taken down from the cross
14. Jesus' body is laid in the tomb

**The Resurrection of Jesus**
On the first day of the week, at the first sign of dawn, the women went to the tomb with the spices they had prepared. They found that the stone had been rolled away from the tomb, but on entering they could not find the body of the Lord Jesus. As they stood there puzzled about this, two men in brilliant clothes suddenly appeared at their side. Terrified, the women bowed their heads to the ground. But the

two said to them, "Why look among the dead for someone who is alive? He is not here; he has risen."
(*Luke 24:1-6a*)

## THE LITANY OF THE SAINTS

| | |
|---|---|
| Lord, have mercy | Lord, have mercy |
| Christ, have mercy | Christ, have mercy |
| Lord, have mercy | Lord, have mercy |

| | |
|---|---|
| Holy Mary, Mother of God | pray for him/her |
| Holy angels of God | pray for him/her |
| Saint Michael, archangel | pray for him/her |
| Saint John the Baptist | pray for him/her |
| St Joseph | pray for him/her |
| Saint Peter and Saint Paul | pray for him/her |
| Saint Patrick | pray for him/her |
| Saint Brigid | pray for him/her |
| Saint Oliver Plunkett | pray for him/her |
| (*Other saints may be included here*) | |
| All holy men and women | pray for him/her |

| | |
|---|---|
| Lord, be merciful | Lord, save your people |
| From all evil | Lord, save your people |
| From every sin | Lord, save your people |
| From Satan's power | Lord, save your people |
| At the moment of death | Lord, save your people |
| From everlasting death | Lord, save your people |
| On the day of judgement | Lord, save your people |
| By your coming as man | Lord, save your people |
| By your suffering and cross | Lord, save your people |

| | |
|---|---|
| By your death and rising to new life | Lord, save your people |
| By your return in the glory of the Father | Lord, save your people |
| By your gift of the Holy Spirit | Lord, save your people |
| By your coming again in glory | Lord, save your people |
| Be merciful to us sinners | Lord, hear our prayer |
| Bring N. to eternal life, first promised to him/her in baptism | Lord, hear our prayer |
| Raise N. on the last day, for he/she has eaten the bread of life | Lord, hear our prayer |
| Let N. share in your glory, for he/she has shared in your suffering and death | Lord, hear our prayer |
| Jesus, Son of the living God | Lord, hear our prayer |
| Christ, hear us | Christ, hear us |
| Lord Jesus, hear our prayer | Lord Jesus, hear our prayer |